A COMMON TRAGEDY

"THE LIFE WE FAIL TO LIVE"

Kenneth Rahal

Printed in the United States of America

First Printing, 2016

Published by
Midnight Cry Ministries
P.O. Box 685
Southern Pines, NC 28388

In obedience to what God has spoken to my heart and from thoughts and circumstances He has applied to my life and some recent books that I have read, may I take those words, thoughts and circumstances and share them with you.

With humility of mind, I pray that no Glory comes my way, but only to Him, who was on the cross.

Kenneth Rahal

"Therefore, if a man cleanses himself from these things, he will be a vessel of honor, sanctified, useful to the Master, prepared for every good work." 2 Timothy 2.21

TABLE OF CONTENTS

FOREWORD

Writing A COMMON TRAGEDY has been a life-changing experience. I wrote it during the most challenging ten years of my life. I starting working on it when I thought I was too sick to begin anything in my life. But our Great and Loving God carried me through this unbelievable journey and Blessed me along the way with His undying Love and His Constant presence.

On June 21, 2006 I was diagnosed with stage four pancreatic cancer and was read a death sentence of 6 to 9 months to live. I had never faced a challenge as this as for 22 years I had been a federal agent with the DEA of the U.S Department of Justice, trusting no one in my life, only my partner, my bullet-proof vest and my weapon and determination to place drug offenders into prison with a punitive attitude opposite of the love and mercy that was about to come into my life.

Even though I had been living a life as "A Convenient Christian," going to church and saying the odd prayer when I wasn't on the golf course, for some reason I had been ignoring the love that God was trying to show me through the years. The death sentence made me feel the need for God in my life. I was raised in a faith where I knew of Jesus but didn't think He knew me as I was taught that I had to go through other intercessors in order to bring my struggles to Him. After a while it felt like a waste of time as I felt He didn't know me.

But for some reason what the doctor said awakened me and caught my attention and, like Paul, I was knocked off my horse, realizing that God had a plan for me that I was ignoring and He needed to get my attention. For some reason I spoke up to the doctor and those present in my hospital room at the moment as I had just returned from the recovery room after undergoing the mother of all surgeries — what is known as "the Whipple procedure," an 11-hour surgery where half of my stomach, my gall bladder, half of my pancreas, 5 feet of my small intestine and my duodenum, as well as the infectious tumor, were removed. I bravely said, "Well, doc, that is a win-win situation." He looked at me and asked what I meant. "I responded and said, "If God leaves me here I have won; if He takes me home I have won so you see, Doc, I can't lose." I weakly got out of bed, walked over to the window and said out loud, "Satan, you can take your pancreatic cancer, your Whipple procedure, your chemo, your radiation and anything else that comes along and go straight back to hell where you belong as you will not steal the joy and love I will receive from my God."

Little did I know the war was about to begin and so was my education in learning who our God really is and the depth of the love He has for me.

The following pages will share my next nine-and-a-half years during which I experienced a total of 9 surgeries, a pancreatic transplant, the cancer spreading to my liver, 3 cyber knife procedures, 23 endoscopies, and a total of 59 admissions to the hospital from 5 weeks to 7 days. On January 5th of this year I was declared "cancer free." To GOD be the GLORY for GREAT things HE has done.

INTRODUCTION

It is amazing to discover, that even though God created man in His image, that every person is a unique creation of God, with their own blend of habits, personality traits, gifts and talents. But there is a common factor that I have observed among Christian brothers and have also seen in my own life.

Perhaps I should change the statement "a common factor" to a more profound word: "A common tragedy." We as Christian men do share a common tragedy in our lives. It is not the sins we commit, as they through our repentance and the redemption of Jesus our Savior are forgiven. The common tragedy we share is this.... "It is the life we fail to live."

Yet we have intentions of being Godly people, but our desire to be such is still not strong enough to follow through with those intentions.

Some of us, however, do want to go beyond playing the role and to move out of spiritual mediocrity. Some call it spiritual growth, others refer to it as spiritual maturity and still others name it Christlikeness. It goes by many different names, but the hope deep inside our "hearts "rings in unison. We share the same desire, as weak or strong that it may be, to step from "the life we fail to live," to having a "heart for the Master's use."

Exactly how do we search out, find or even experience this Godliness or move from a "life we fail to live" to having a "heart for the Master's use."

For some of us, it is a gradual forward movement of growing and learning. For all of us it is aligning ourselves with His will and when choosing between two roads, we must ask "Which road will contribute more to the kingdom of God."

I have asked myself that question many times, but until recently I never took adequate time to hear the answer. I had always believed that I was as significant to God's plan as a cloudy day. I was about to find out how wrong I was and how deceived I had allowed myself to be all these years.

I thought the scripture read, "I can do all things through Ken Rahal who strengthens me." How soon I was about to see that isn't what it says at all, in fact very much different.

I believed I was strong and needed no one to tell or show me that my attitude in my inconsistencies of my commitments was heading me to a road of destruction.

It was my "road to Damascus" that I was about to experience. Like He did with Paul, the Lord showed His love for me in a way that I never expected. He knocked me off of my horse and put me to the ground in one quick motion. I found myself in an unwanted divorce and then an illness that I never anticipated. Remember, I thought I was strong and that nothing could touch me. Many friends had backed away from me during the divorce and now with the illness I stood before Him, naked, with one thought in mind and a loneliness that made me realize .... "That I never knew how much I needed God, until God was all I had."

I was reminded of the movie "Castaway" in which Tom Hanks played the one stranded on an island, with no hope of being rescued and no hope of communicating with anyone. After a while that changed. In his loneliness and in his despair to talk with someone, he met "Wilson." Being alone with Wilson I can appreciate. Being alone with God, I needed. His plan for my life was finally about to be revealed as I had no choice but to finally hear and listen to His voice. I didn't have a soccer ball in front of me named "Wilson," I had the true, real live, loving God.

May I share 2 Timothy 1:12 with you at this moment, then perhaps you may have a better understanding of what you are about to read and the person who is sharing this with you. It reads "for this reason I also suffer these things, but I am not ashamed, for I know whom I have believed and I am convinced that He is able to guard what I have entrusted to Him until that day."

The words "for I know whom I have believed," are in the past tense, so let me put you in the present because this is where all of this begins. I did not have a history of total commitment to God and a total knowledge of Him until, like Paul, "my road to Damascus." I am going to change the word "know" to "amazed."

As each day goes by and my despair lessens, my coming to know God is a total amazement of His love, His patience, His kindness and His faithfulness to stand and reveal Himself to me and replace the empty loneliness that I had felt each day and remove the physical pain and replace it with His strength and love, but most of all His presence in my life.

I am amazed that as each day goes by, I am fascinated by the God that I am learning to walk with and amazed at His closeness. The suffering that I had experienced, even though much of it was brought on by my own hand, lessens each day and is preoccupied by this amazement of a God, that I never knew existed to the degree that He does.

In the Living Bible, Ephesians 1:18 reads, "I pray that the eyes of your heart will be opened, so that you will see part of the future He has called you to share."

God has given that vision to me but again in a way I never anticipated. Through His body of believers. Through brothers and sisters who share His love and have taught me that we are children of the Father and therefore we are family. We may be rebellious children at times, and even disobedient and sinful, but we are God's children and family and nobody can take that away from us. I have felt a closeness from them, that when I was weeping, they were tasting salt. No judgment, no criticism, just Godly advice and a commitment to prayer. I give Him the glory for what I have learned from them as they breathed into me new life through their prayers and love. To put it plainly … they saved my life.

As I continue to share my heart and experience with you, I want it to be an encouragement to all who read, to realize that God knows that we have faith, but He wants more. He wants our trust. Trust to put Him in every aspect of our life. To place Him into the depths of our hearts, in all things we do and say both in private and in public. To know in our hearts, that even though we may not always understand what He does in our lives, it does not give us reason not to trust Him.

It is my hope for you to hear the words that God is speaking to your hearts, that they become alive with His purpose and powerful in bringing about His will: to be willing to hear His call for you to draw near to Him and to step out of the comfort of mediocrity and to step up to the challenge of a closer daily walk with Him, so that daily simple obedience to Him becomes second nature to you; to strengthen your hearts and to bring truth, integrity and character into the very middle of your lives.

When it comes to spiritual growth and maturity, I have felt at times a bit of frustration. Like I'm at a large table with friends and family, poring over a giant jigsaw puzzle, looking for that one little piece that will unlock the door to the other four thousand nine hundred and ninety-nine pieces. Others seem to be excited about the discoveries they're making by finding the correct pieces, while I'm still struggling to find the elusive corner piece that will give me hope. So I quietly excuse myself and retire to another room to participate in an activity that I enjoy…like reading a good book. At least with a good book, a person can go from a lack of clarity and understanding, to a complete picture that is unfolded one paragraph at a time. Sometimes a book includes suspense and intrigue, but for me that just adds to the expectation and anticipation.

Or maybe it's feeling like Dr. Watson, that well known sidekick of Sherlock Holmes, that great mystery solver. He always seems to be able to pull all the pieces of the murder puzzle together while we are the last ones to figure it out, even when we have been with Sherlock every step of the way.

It is my belief that the Christian life was never meant to be as frustrating as a jigsaw puzzle or so complex that I am destined to live in the shadow of the great spiritual mystery solvers. There's no denying it, there will always be those things that I do not fully comprehend (after all we are called to walk by faith). But I believe that God has intended that even the youngest Christian be able to grow and mature spiritually. In fact, I would go as far to say that it is even possible for a young child to mature in the things of Christ.

For you see, God has provided the means for Spiritual Growth. It's not an unsolvable mystery or a massive jigsaw puzzle. We have everything we need to experience the wonder and joy of a growing, dynamic relationship with Jesus Christ. Once we surrender to Him, we can look back to see how far we have grown in the things of the Lord. We can solve the mystery and complete the puzzles, because unlike the puzzles at our dining room table, we have ALL THE PIECES NECESSARY.

Why is it that we Christian men are often content to be saved, slip into church on Sunday, slump down, slumber and slither out at the appointed time (whether the service is over or not)? Why are we so willing to be spectators in the Kingdom and consign ourselves to that life as previously mentioned of Spiritual mediocrity? We come to church and hear the things of God, we see the things of God and we learn the things of God who stands before us and says "let me reveal my Glory to you." Yet with all of that, we choose to stand on the sidelines and catch only a glimpse of Him as He passes by. We acknowledge Him as our Savior, yet we stand in a place of mediocrity and we reduce His glory. We choose to be players sitting on the bench and not on the field in the game.

Wouldn't it be more exciting to be in the middle of the action, placing ourselves in the center of God's work in this world? Yet most of us remain firmly planted on the sidelines.

Why don't we get up and get involved?

Well, "I'm not the kind of guy who likes to get involved," is a comment that is heard regularly. It usually comes from a man who is trying to be honest. He doesn't see himself as being an extroverted, high-energy, big splash sort of a guy. I appreciate his candor, but a closer look may reveal another side of this quiet brother.

The truth is, all of us are aggressive about many things … do you relate to any of the following?

POLITICS … The mere mention of that word can set the shyest person off on a tirade about who's right and what's wrong in this country.

VOCATION … Here's a great example of involvement. One of our goals as a man is to discover our vocational calling in life and then pursue it with vigor.

SPORTS … Ok, it's a male cliché, but it really is true. I know guys, and so do you, who sit quietly in most other contexts, but put them in a stadium or in front of a television showing their favorite team in action and they nearly climb the walls with the excitement of being involved in the game, not to mention knowing much more than the coach about what their team should be doing.

MUSIC … Want to know how to divide a room quickly? Ask people to clarify their personal tastes in music. This is especially dangerous in a Christian setting. There have been Churches who have split up over the issue of "contemporary" music versus "traditional" music. This topic generates plenty of energy, passion and conviction. I just wish it wasn't at the price of unity.

SPIRITUAL GROWTH … Ok, I tried to sneak this one past you. Granted, this is not something we normally think of when we consider aggressive active participation .... but I hope I can change your point of view.

Before we go too far in discussing what Godliness or Christlikeness really means, it might be wise to point out a common misconception. So let me share a personal experience with you.

Growing up in a church in Canada, I was able to observe dozens of well-intentioned men of God, who unintentionally led me down a path of confusion concerning this matter.

As a baby Christian, if you had asked me what a Godly man looks like, I could have described him for you in microscopic detail based on my observations.

He was, first off, a Super Saint.

He had to be a guy who brought a Bible to church. The Bible had to be as thick as a Toronto phone book. Once the Bible was opened, every page was well worn and underlined with a variety of colored felt pens.

Even without his Bible opened, this Super saint could quote scripture from memory. Not just a verse here or there, this guy could recite whole chapters with his eyes closed! He was a biblical database. He could talk about Calvin and Luther like he just had lunch with them the other day. He would pray aloud in church. Each prayer would be filled with "thee's" and "thou's" and "whithersoever thou goest's" to the point that most of us had no idea what our brother was saying.

His clothing left something to be desired. Whatever was in style at the time, this guy wasn't wearing it. After all, we're supposed to be separate from the world, which looked to me that Godliness went hand in hand with the thrift store.

Maybe you are not feeling fulfilled in your life currently. There isn't an experiencing of the abundant life that Jesus described in the Gospels. This may not be happening for you in some areas of your life, but you see it in others. Perhaps you feel guilty, because you are not the Super saint that was described above. You are stressing because you feel you don't read your Bible enough or pray as you think you should. You want to do these things, but you haven't quite figured out how to get it together. Quite honestly, it appears sometimes completely overwhelming. How can a man move his heart toward God anyway?

How can a man have "a heart for the Master's use"?

In describing what it means to have "a heart for the Master's use," the best place to begin is in the scriptures. The apostle Paul has one of the best summary statements on this issue in the Bible. Tucked away in prison, Paul wrote these words to the church in Philippi: "That I may know Him and the power of His resurrection and the fellowship of His sufferings, being conformed to His death." Phil. 3:10.

The key to that verse are the words "know Him." What does it mean to know Christ? One thing for certain, the word Paul uses for knowledge means a great more than accumulating statistical and factual information. It is an intimate relationship with Christ that draws us closer to Him. It is the simple obedience to draw near to God when He calls and say to Him, "Lord, I am available."

It is the beginning of a journey that begins with a superficial relationship, to one of complete intimacy.

Let me give you a suggestion.

Think of someone close in your life. Could it be that person is your spouse? There would be no human more intimate with you than her.

11

When you first met and began to see each other, there was a bit of learning about one another in terms of where you had grown up, the number of brothers and sisters, what kind of foods you liked, the kinds of music you enjoyed and things like that.

The "facts" are helpful in beginning to frame a relationship. But as time progressed and you continued to see each other, you began to see your spouse to be in a different light. You wanted to get to know her even better and that was not an intellectual pursuit. It wasn't just the technical and factual knowledge about her that moved you to grow in love with her. It was being in her presence, experiencing her, getting to know how she thinks, feels and reacts to life that drew you to her. It was the process of moving from the truth about her, to a place of action.

It is this sort of experimental knowledge, the intimacy of the heart and life that draws us closer to God as well. But, like getting to know your mate, knowing Christ follows a pattern that moves us from the more superficial levels of friendship, into a relationship of intimacy.

There are some men that I know, of whom I must say that I was envious of their relationship with the Lord. But as I began to say, Lord, I am available, I began to realize that these men were ordinary and God was using them because they were available.

The scriptures give us a closer look at such a thought. Let's look more closely at some men of the Bible. Men who I must say are my heroes. They weren't perfect plaster statues on pedestals. They were real live flesh and blood guys, complete with shortcomings and imperfections. Yet they were used mightily of God and had "a heart for the Master's use."

Consider a few examples:

NOAH … Nothing seemed out of the ordinary about this man until the earth was flooded. The only way of rescue, was the ark he had built in obedience to God's command.

GIDEON … At one point he was hiding in fear. Then God called him to defeat Israel's enemies and restore its freedom.

DAVID … In weak moments, he could commit adultery and murder. Yet for most of his life, he was a man after God's own heart.

NEHEMIAH … He served in the house of a pagan king, yet God used him to lead the entire nation of Israel in rebuilding the walls around Jerusalem.

JOB … His is the classic story of a regular guy who loved God and was put through trials beyond belief. He dared to question God, but still he said, "Though He slay me; yet will I trust Him."

PETER … Talk about an average guy. Here was a man who constantly struggled with his temper. Usually speaking without thinking (opening his mouth just long enough to take one foot out and put the other in) and with a variety of other shortcomings. Yet he also became an apostle and was the author of two books of the Bible.

PAUL … Before his conversion, he zealously persecuted God's people. Afterward he could enjoy the joy of the Lord, while enduring the pain of imprisonment for his faith.

What is the common factor arching over all of these men? Was it that once in a while they would take themselves from their daily work and responsibilities and allow God to use some of their time? I don't think so. The desire to know Him as Paul spoke about earlier in Philippians had become a consuming passion in their lives.

In the Old Testament, they were motivated by the Lord's faithfulness in His promises. In the New Testament, it was the "personal relationship" they had developed with Jesus Christ after the revelation of the fulfillment of the prophesies concerning His death and resurrection. They were motivated by the faithfulness of God. It created a passion in them as it can in you, to have that feeling inside that moves you from the bench to the playing field. You then become a player in the game and are motivated to become a winner in God's kingdom.

This is called Spiritual growth. This is called surrendering ourselves to His leadership.

This is called having "a heart for the Master's Use."

What is this "motivation" that helps us to move from a place of mediocrity to a place of action. Is it a feeling we finally come to, or is it a spoken word or voice that gives us that motivation?

Let me give you an example of how we can be in an impossible situation, but all it takes is a "spoken" word to motivate us into action.

Imagine you are walking home late one night and decided to take a shortcut through a cemetery. In the darkness, you stumble and fall into an open grave. You yell for help until your voice grows faint from the strain. No matter how loudly you scream, no one is there to help you out. You try climbing out of the grave, but the walls are too steep and it is too deep of a hole. Your arms and legs are weak from exhaustion. Completely worn out, you decide to sit in a dark corner of the grave, waiting until the cemetery workers show up in the morning.

A short time later, another guy who wanted to take a short cut falls into the same open grave totally unaware you are there. Just like you, he begins screaming for help and trying with all of his might, yet without success to climb out of the grave. Trying to be helpful and being unseen from the dark corner of the grave, you say in your low tired voice "you can't get out of here." But hearing this voice and not knowing where it came from he was instantly motivated and "he did get out of there."

It's all about motivation and a spoken word.

Unfortunately, it's possible to be motivated to do the right thing and yet use the wrong method. That's apparently what was happening in the churches in the region known as Galatia in New Testament times. The apostle Paul had to write them in order to correct their methodology. They had adopted a method that has come to be known today as Galatianism. Simply put, Galatianism is the mistaken belief that we can grow in Godliness through legalism, that is, through following a set of rules. We can take the good things, the tools that God gives us, parts of scripture and resources and bring ourselves into a system of works and law keeping.

As Paul instructed the Galatian believers, we don't pursue Spiritual growth in Godliness through our own efforts, but through the empowerment of God's grace through a total surrender to a personal sold-out relationship with Jesus Christ and a desire to know Him. That is a point worth addressing, because in the long run, it is that point that produces motivation to Godly living.

"I have been crucified with Christ; and it is no longer I who live, but Christ who lives in me; and the life which I now live in the flesh, I live by faith in the Son of God, who loved me and gave Himself up for me. I do not nullify the Grace of God, for if righteousness comes through the law, then Christ died needlessly." Galatians 2:20-21.

Because of learning and listening to what God was saying to me in my own conflicts, I can tell you that it's a passion that will fuel our desire to have "a heart for the Master's use" and that our pursuit is through God's grace.

Now let's get practical. It may sound a bit selfish, but it's still valid to ask concerning Spiritual growth, what's in it for me? Why should I pursue Godliness? The apostle Paul wrote, "but have nothing to do with worldly fables fit only for old women. On the other hand, discipline yourself for the purpose of Godliness; for bodily discipline is only of little profit, but Godliness is profitable for all things, since it holds promise for the present life and also for the life to come." 1 Timothy 4:7-8

I don't know many people who will give themselves to something until they know and understand the benefits. So let's look at the real benefits of Godliness and Spiritual growth. No false advertising. As sergeant Joe Friday would say on the old Dragnet T.V. show, "Just the facts."

As we look at the benefits of being involved in Spiritual growth, realize that this list is by no means exhaustive, but, as it has for me, should stimulate your thinking in the right direction so that you will have a deeper understanding when Jesus said, "I came that they may have life, and have it abundantly."

Believe me, I can tell you, He never intended for us to struggle on our own, hoping that one day we would make it to glory and then experience fullness of life. No. He promised us the abundant life that is a foretaste of glory, here and now.

Spiritual growth always brings blessings. It's a basic principle that is deeply rooted in the Scriptures.

Let me share with you a few examples and thoughts that God placed on my heart for my own direction.

CONSISTENCY IN LIFE … Stability! I can't think of anything worse than fishing in a small boat on the ocean when it has big waves. Life doesn't have to feel that way though. Noah was a wonderful example of a man who didn't allow life to overwhelm him. In a time of great wickedness on earth, he remained consistent in his devotion to God, working for 120 years to build an ark according to God's command. Or what about the psalmist in the 1st Psalm. His image of a tree planted by a source of nourishment so the roots can go deep and withstand the storms of life is a wonderful picture of consistency.

INTEGRITY … Integrity means that what's on the outside is a reflection of what's inside. It's the real substance of a man. Daniel illustrates this quality beautifully. When an order went forth that the people were only to pray in the name of Babylon's King Darius, Daniel went to his upstairs room where the windows were open, got down on his knees and prayed to the God of heaven 3 times a day … as he had been doing previously. There was no false show, but rather a simple living out of what was on the inside. His daily simple obedience to God, had become second nature to him. It's interesting to note that not one negative thing is said about him in scripture.

CHARACTER … Spiritual growth will produce character as well. Character means many things, but one thing included in its definition is that we can be trusted. Let me share with you a story I read from Promise Keepers, as I believe it certainly applies to this issue.

There was a young man who applied for a position with a firm. As he was about to be interview by the VP, the interviewer said the following.

"Before I ask you any questions, please write on this piece of paper, three words that would best describe your character. But before you write them, I want you to know that I have contacted your references and have asked them to do the same thing and I have their answers at this time." The core of this little story is if someone was to have you describe your character in three words, would one of those words be Godly. Would others or yourself consider you to be a Godly man?

DEEPER RELATIONSHIPS … When we pursue Spiritual growth, we can also enjoy a deeper relationship with God and with family, friends and co-workers. The intimacy David had with God is seen throughout the many psalms he wrote. The fact is, that there is more written about him in scripture than there is about anyone else besides Jesus. On a couple of occasions, God even called him a man after His own heart.

STRONGER THOUGHT LIFE … The Bible, through the apostle Paul, calls us to "take captive" every thought to the glory of Christ.

The majority of Christian men that I know don't face serious struggles over what they do in their lives, whether it's from positive peer pressure or fear of the consequences of sin.

As I did in my own life, they control their actions most of the time. But I can tell you as they, that controlling our thought life is another matter. As we develop "a heart for the Master's use" God will enable us to take captive our thoughts ... "and the peace of God, which surpasses all comprehension, will guard your hearts and your minds in Christ Jesus. Finally brethren, whatever is true, whatever is honorable, whatever is right, whatever is pure, whatever is lovely, whatever is of good repute, if there is any excellence and if anything worthy of praise, dwell on these things." Philippians 4:7-8.

IMPROVED BUSINESS LIFE ... Pursuing Spiritual growth can also improve your business lives. By that I mean, they can give you a moral compass that enables us to navigate the treacherous waters so often present in our business situations. As we draw closer to Christ it doesn't mean everything forever after will be great, or we'll never lose a job, our bosses will always appreciate us, our companies will consistently be profitable and so on, but we will know what we are doing and why we are doing it. We'll have the moral compass necessary to navigate in a world filled with a variety of obstacles and that will give us the encouragement to bring Christ into the business world.

As we seek to have "a heart for the Master's use," it is my prayer and desire for you that you would be at the point in your relationship with God, to have Him look down upon you, put His arms around you and say as He did to David many centuries ago, "You are a man after my own heart." That will be success. There will be no regrets. That is the kind of life that has a positive impact on the world, that leaves a legacy for our families, our church and our community. There are many benefits to pursuing the Godly life through Spiritual growth. As we move into this sharing or study, let me state something that I have learned over the past months. Yes, it is true that through my own hand I have lost everything. But in my restoration and through God's love, I have learned what a truly successful man is.

"A successful man is one who can stand before anyone, anywhere at any time, and say from the bottom of his heart, to the Glory of God the Father, that His Son, Jesus Christ is Lord."

That my brothers, is a successful man. That my brothers, is a man who has a "heart for the Master's use, "in his Bible reading, in his prayer life, in his praise and worship and in his communicating his faith."

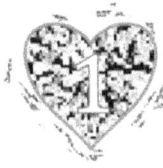

A HEART...FOR THE MASTER'S USE...IS A HEART FOR THE BIBLE

Many of us men have tons of good intentions when it comes to reading the Bible, but for a number of reasons, we just don't get around to it consistently. I don't say this to generate guilt. I'm just admitting that there are many of us who have the same identical struggles.

Do you love God's Word? One would think that every man would answer in the affirmative the following. The Bible is our life, our strength, our joy. Yet statistics indicate that only about ten percent of Christian men read their Bible every day. More fall into the category of "once in a while" while others only look at it when the pastor preaches from it on Sunday morning or they are faced with a major crisis. A fair question, then, is why should we love the Scriptures? David took that very issue in some of the comments he penned in Psalm 119.

"May your failing love come to me O Lord, your salvation according to your promise; then I will answer the one who taunts me, for I trust in your word. Do not snatch the word of truth from my mouth, for I have put my hope in your laws. I will always obey your laws, forever and ever. I will walk about in freedom, for I have sought out your precepts. I will speak of your statutes before kings and will not be put to shame, for I delight in your commandments, which I love, and I meditate on your decrees." Psalm 119:41-48.

If you are like me, and until recently I was not there, your eye is drawn to this phrase in that wonderful text: "I delight in your commandments because I love them." I questioned how David could have used such intimate terms. The text offers some reasons why we, as he did, should all love the Word of God.

It proclaims God's mercies and salvation.

According to the Bible, salvation comes from the Word of God. It is the incorruptible seed that lives and abides forever. But I believe David was going even further than that statement because of his reference to, "may your unfailing love come to me." That's a common theme in the Bible, as seen in another psalm: "The Lord is gracious and compassionate, slow to anger and rich in love. The Lord is good to all; He has compassion on all He has made." Psalm 145:8-9.

I guess you can see now why I do love those words. They proclaim love and forgiveness. That is what David needed, that is what I needed.

During my life and because of my failures, I viewed God as the deity sitting up in heaven holding a baseball bat, ready to club me for every false move that I made, not only hating my sins, but hating me as well. This misconception was causing me to try to make myself look good, manipulating for approval in all that I did, right or wrong. "With or without God's love, I am going to make myself look the best I can."

But I have learned, as I hope you can, that he is compassionate to all. He understands who we are and gives us grace, rather than what we deserve. Whatever happens in our lives, from overflowing toilets to traffic jams to credit cards over the limits, it's good to remind ourselves that God is so good. By dwelling on that thought, He will often keep us from getting into even more trouble. What a wonderful reason to love the Word of God … to simply learn more of His mercy and His salvation, but most of all, as I need to hear, HIS LOVE.

It promises freedom.

The most tied-up troubled Christians, I know, because I was one of them, are those who either ignore God's Word or misuse it. Perhaps they follow the traditions and opinions of men, or maybe, as I did, they talk the good talk, but they end up in bondage to themselves. The good news however, is that "the word sets us free." Paul told the Corinthians, "Now the Lord is the Spirit, and where the Spirit of the Lord is, there is freedom. And we, who with unveiled faces all reflect the Lord's glory, are being transformed into His likeness with ever-increasing glory, which comes from the Lord, who is the Spirit." 2 Corinthians 3:17-18.

Where do we see the glory of God? In the Word! As we are being transformed into His likeness, one of the results is liberty. This gets me very excited. The more we allow the glory of God to saturate our minds and hearts through reading the Word, the more it sets us free to be all that God wants us to be. As I mentioned earlier, we come to church, we hear the things of God, we learn the things of God and we see the things of God.

With that, He stands before us and says, "Let me show you My glory." Yet we step back and catch only a glimpse of Him as He walks by … the life we fail to live … such a tragedy. What God was wanting to show us was all the joy we have ever wanted, all the peace we have wanted to have, and His forgiveness as well.

These do not come by putting a veil over our faces, which in Paul's words symbolizes indirect access to God. Rather we are able to go directly to the Word to experience His glorious freedom. Jesus told the people in John 8:36 that the truth would set them free and that, "if the Son sets you free, you will be free indeed." I can tell you from my own experience, by spending time in the Bible, we're set free from wrong thinking, discouragement, wrong attitudes and especially wrong actions.

The more we know the Word, the greater freedom we'll experience.

God speaks to us.

The most basic aspect of spending time in the Scriptures, is simply to read them. I suggest that you find a translation that is comfortable to you. I presently use the NASB but the paraphrased Living Bible in it's simple language has helped me to see that God's message to me is personal and not general as the following story will show you.

I love to fish. Especially on a pier at the ocean. When I walk out onto the pier, there is a common feeling with everyone to encourage each other "to catch a lot or even the big one." As I am walking to a selected spot on the rail, I pass several people and say several times, "Hey guys, how's the fishing?"

Well, in the Living Bible, there is a passage where Jesus is walking along the sea shore after His Glorious Resurrection, and He sees

Peter and the others in the boat and what does He do, but calls out to them and says, "Hey boys, how is the fishing?" Tell me God's Word is not alive. Tell me it is not personal.

Tell me He doesn't have a message for each of us through a book that was not just inspired for the masses, but before creation was, a message that would be placed in our individual hearts, alive with His purpose, and powerful in bringing about His will in our lives.

The Bible is reading as you would a novel, a biography or a book from a Christian book store. It's reading for education. It's reading for enlightenment. It's reading for enjoyment. In the Old Testament, I have found it to be about a nation and its people. In the New Testament, I have found it to be about a man and the undying love He has for us.

It is a journey where as we travel through its pages, we allow God to speak to us, ever so quietly.

For many of us, this kind of reading is part of a daily important routine called a quiet time. Thus it's a wonderful idea to do it consistently. Now the last thing I want to do is throw guilt around. Reading the Word is a great way to focus our thoughts on Spiritual things, so the more often we do it, the better. "Finally brethren, whatever is true, whatever is honorable, whatever is right, whatever is pure, whatever is lovely, whatever is of good repute, if there is any excellence and if anything worthy of praise, let your mind dwell on these things. The things you have learned and received and heard and seen in me, practice these things; and the God of peace shall be with you." Philippians 4:8-9.

If you are a morning person, try beginning each day with a few minutes in His Word. It has taken me sixty-three years to realize that there is no better way to start a day, each day, than with a good cup of coffee and the Word of God. I look forward to getting up early in the morning like 5:30, put the coffee on and be talking to God while doing this. I shared earlier that fellowship with God had become a reality to me. Yes, I can putter around in the kitchen, putting the coffee on, or sit on the sofa in my den with a coffee in hand and have a conversation with Him.

But the most important part of that togetherness is when He speaks to me from His Word and He always does. I end the day in the same manner. That is my time also for prayer and the reading of a good Christian book.

Some guys spend their lunch hour with the Lord, others their afternoon coffee break. Find the time of the day that works best for you, then go for it. I want to stress an important point to you. It's not the end of the world if you don't read the Bible every day.

I know some guys who have stopped reading their Bible completely, because they missed a day here and there. If you can only squeeze in a day or two each week with the Word, that's alright for now, do it! Your schedule may vary from week to week or month to month or you may be in a particularly busy period at present but that's ok. Perhaps in a month or two, a larger window of time will open up for you, but begin to read today. I share this truth with you. I have found that the more I read it, and so will you, the more I want to read it, every day. It will become your delight.

Returning to our look at Psalm 119, if we truly love God's Word, we can expect to see at least three different responses flowing out of our lives. Obedience … Joy … Trust ….

Obedience.

In the heart of the text we observed earlier, we find this statement. "I will always obey your law, for ever and ever." People who love God's Word are dedicated to obeying Him. I have found that as I read daily, that simple, daily obedience to Him, begins and has now become second nature to me as it will you.

Joy.

In the first Psalm, we are told that Godly men will delight in the Word day and night, meditating on it constantly. Men who have a heart for the Bible delight in it. Nothing is more important to them and as a result, it brings joy to the very center of their lives.

Trust.

Loving the Word, I have learned, teaches us to depend on what it says. "I reach out my hands for your commandments, which I love, and I meditate on your decrees." Lifting up one's hands to receive what God wants to give to us is a powerful symbol of complete dependence on the Lord. I remember my own daughter when she was a little child, often reaching up to me with her hands for my love and to place her on my lap to hear what I would want to say to her or to read her a story from her favorite book.

It illustrates a man who trusts God with his life. The palms are open and not clenched. The fingers are pointed upwards indicating all that comes to us in life, comes from the Lord. The more I learn about God from His Word, the more I want to trust Him as so will you.

"How Blessed is the man who has made the Lord his trust." Psalm 40:5.

I will ask you one simple question. Do you love God's Word? If so, may I suggest demonstrating that love by cultivating this all-important area of Spiritual growth and by spending time in it.

J.L. Packer wrote insightfully about an effective strategy of Satan concerning our relationship with our Bible, God's Word. "If I were the devil, one of my first aims would be to stop men from reading and experiencing the truth of the Bible. Knowing that it is the Word of God, teaching men to know, love and serve the Living God of the Word, I would do all that I could to surround it with the Spiritual equivalent of pits, interruptions, thorn hedges and man traps to frighten people off … and at all costs want to keep them from using their minds in a disciplined way to get the fullness of its message."

Brothers, I have lived the reality that the enemy's purpose is to kill, steal and destroy.

Men, let us secure a course to avoid those traps.

Let us develop a heart for the Bible.

Let us develop "a heart for the Master's use."

PERSONAL REFLECTIONS

What do I think what God is asking of me as to my time reading the Bible?

Am I taking time to hear what He is saying to me?

Am I willing to move from "Mediocrity" to "having a Heart for the Master's use"?

How will I do this?

Am I willing to share this experience with others?

NOTES

A HEART ... FOR THE MASTER'S USE ... IS A HEART FOR PRAYER

It's a television program I will never forget.

I don't even remember the speaker's name, but I remember the couple of minutes I saw of him while channel surfing one evening. My trusted remote control in hand, I was zipping through all the channels when I stumbled upon a television church service. I normally don't watch church on television, but I was fascinated by the fact that the preacher had a telephone beside him on the pulpit. Why would this guy have a phone beside him? I was about to receive my answer.

"I want to talk to you today about the topic of prayer," the pastor began softly. I still didn't get the connection with the phone. "Prayer is just another way of saying we are having a conversation with God," he continued. "When was the last time you spoke with the Lord?" Fortunately for my conscience, I had just talked with the Lord a short time before, so I didn't need to feel guilty. "I've heard people say they don't talk to God because they are just too shy to approach Him. Well, I can understand your feelings. But I want you to understand a couple of points. First, God is always accessible. You need not feel intimidated to approaching Him. As a matter of fact, He wants to talk with you. Second, even the shyest people I know have no problem talking on the phone. They can pick up the receiver and talk to their friends for hours." With that, he picked up the phone and held it out towards the camera. "God is your friend. He wants to talk with you. Why don't you pick up the phone and talk to Him right now."

Now I confess, it was a little corny, but the image stuck with me. This guy had prayer nailed down tight. When we sweep away all the Spiritual sounding jargon, prayer is the wonderful privilege of carrying on an extended conversation with the Living Lord. Prayer is one of most enjoyable moments of Spiritual growth. Men often neglect it, however, and the reasons are difficult to identify. To say it is a lack of training is an oversimplification. Prayer is not simply a ritual that happens at a prescribed time and precise place, using a predetermined format. Through prayer, God leaves the pages of history and is experienced as a present reality. He is more than just Jesus the historical hero. He is someone we talk to in the current moment! May I share with you how to take a closer look and make talking to God a more practical and accessible part of our lives. If you have noticed, I have said "talking with God" and not "to God." Let us refer back to 1 John 1:7. The word "with" is in that text and what I have learned from this is "with" is a two-person conversation.

The benefits of prayer.

Why should we as men pray? Are there advantages? From the testimony I previously shared with you, prayer is what helped me begin to hear and see the plan and calling that God has placed on my life. Consider just a few of these advantages that I have felt … peace of mind … purity of heart … desire for service … purpose in life …presence of joy … prevention of temptation.

It's hard to imagine that we not only have the privilege of talking directly with our Heavenly Father, but He also rewards us with an impressive list of results.

The key to effective prayer.

The key to effective prayer is discussed in two separate passages written by the apostle John. Consider these words. "Whatever you ask in My name, that will I do, so that the Father may be glorified in the Son. If you ask anything in My name, I will do it." John 14:13-14.

"This is the confidence which we have before Him, that if we ask anything according to His will, He hears us. And if we know that He hears us in whatever we ask, we know that we have the requests which we have asked from Him." 1 John 5:14-15.

If we were to sum up those two verses in one distinct statement, it would be this: "Prayer really works. It will make a difference in your life. I can guarantee it because God guarantees it. I can guarantee it, because I have experienced it.

Let me share with you a helpful method I recently learned in how to structure my prayers. It is simple and is a good model to follow. It begins with the word … ACTS … as an acronym.

A … Adoration.

Begin your prayer with praise for the Lord. Thank Him for His greatness. Spend a few minutes communicating to Him how much you love Him. Isn't it amazing that He is so great, yet so accessible.

C … Confession.

The second aspect of prayer is cleansing yourself before Him. Admit to God your shortcomings, confess your sins and ask for His forgiveness. This is a wonderfully therapeutic part of Christian prayer. The apostle John tells us that if we confess our sins, he will forgive them.

T … Thanksgiving.

The third part of prayer is fun! Think of all the things that God has done for you and give thanks for them. In my turmoil, I have come away from prayer so incredibly encouraged, because I spent time giving thanks for the many blessings.

S … Supplication.

Finally bring all your requests to the Lord. I found it was necessary for me to start spending a little more time in the first three aspects as in the beginning of my fellowship with Him, my prayers were characterized by a barrage of gimme, gimme, gimmie's.

This is not a magical formula. I have found myself saying and I am sure so do other men, "If my requests are always God's will, I will always receive what I have asked for, so why do I even need to ask God for things, since He already knows what I need."

The best answer I can give you is from scripture and my heart in understanding this scripture. Let us go to Romans 8:28, 29, and 30.

"And we know that God causes all things to work together for good to those who love God, to those who are called to His purpose. For whom He foreknew, He also predestined to become conformed to the image of His Son, that He might be the first born among many brethren; and these whom He predestined, He also called; and these whom He called, He also justified; and these whom He justified, He also glorified." The tense of this scripture shows, that as Godly Men, our future glorification is so certain that it can be said to be accomplished. In other words, our mansion in heaven has already been built and our name is on the door post. What is missing is us. The Father has not yet called us home.

What knowledge to have, what security to live with. What inner assurance this is.

However, we must maintain an intimacy with Him and live each day as if we were living in our mansion and our conduct must be as such, that we cannot allow ourselves with this security to fall back into mediocrity.

When we pray, or should I say "talk" with God consistently, intimacy with Him is developed. Let me give you an illustration of intimacy. Earlier I described developing a relationship with your wife so let us presume that now being married and committed to your marriage you come home to her each day after a rough day on the job. Because of that intimacy with her, she intuitively knows you have had a bad day as soon as you drag your weary body through the door. But deeper intimacy is developed between you when you invite her into your world by talking about what took place. The sharing, the emotions and the communication all add up to an important result.

It's no longer "your" day, but it now becomes "our" day. It's not just about "you," it is now about ''us.'' As it works with your wife, so it works the same way with God. He delights in hearing us recount the highs and lows of our day. It draws us closer to the

Father as we develop an even greater intimacy with Him, by opening up to Him.

There's awesome power in prayer.

The only weak link is our faith and our trust in His word that "all the promises of God find their yes in Christ." 2 Cor. 1:20.

We must allow Him to strengthen this weak link if it is there, for when we develop an intimacy with God, we begin a relationship with Him that allows our prayer life to emulate that of His Son and find our yes in Him.

We can think God's thoughts.

"But He turned and said to Peter, get behind Me, Satan! You are a stumbling block to Me; for you are not setting your mind on God's interests, but man's." Matt. 16:23.

Peter thought the way man thought, not in the way God thought. He saw the immediate problem, but did not discover how that problem fit into God's over all thinking. In order to think God's thoughts, we must be prepared to go beyond the limits of mere human thinking. This does not mean we become foolish or illogical, it just means that we submit our thinking to His wisdom, which is higher than our own human reason. That doesn't mean we see and understand a situation as fully as God does.

So how can we think God's thoughts so that we can experience more yes answers to our prayers? By realizing that His thoughts seldom concern us alone. He thinks about us in relations to others. So, as I have had to do, keep your eyes and ears open to see if He is saying the same thing to others. It's one of the surest ways to confirm His word to us and to truly know if at times it is God's voice we are hearing. Jesus said, "If two or more of you agree on earth about anything they ask, it will be done by My Father in Heaven." Matt. 18:19. It isn't agreeing on our thoughts that bring yes answers to our prayers, but agreeing on His thoughts.

We can feel God's emotions.

The Bible is clear on this matter. God is tenderhearted and compassionate. He hates the sin, but loves the sinner. Jesus wept over Jerusalem. The angels rejoice when a sinner repents. People and angels share God's emotions.

When Nehemiah heard about the desolation of the holy city of Jerusalem, he sat down and wept for days. God does not take seriously those who do not share His feelings. "This people honors me with their lips, but their heart is far from Me." Matt. 15:8. This certainly is a reflection of my past. If we are to have intimacy with God in our prayers, then we must not only think with Him, we must feel with Him.

We can desire God's plan.

We can think of God's thoughts and feel God's emotions, but still stand on the sidelines as on observer and not a player ... "the life we fail to live...

This is the step of personal commitment. This is where God's thoughts and emotions become our personal concern. We not only know what God knows and feel what he feels, but now we want what God wants. Men, I plead with you to understand how important it is to get off the bench and into the game and become deeply involved in the plans of God, so that when we pray, "Thy kingdom come, Thy will be done" … it is not a prayer that we learned just from memory but a prayer that becomes a consuming passion in our lives. In fact, THE consuming passion in our lives.

We can speak God's words.

Thinking, feeling, desiring … we think of these as being essentially silent expressions, even though as we have seen, they involve real commitment. But there comes a point when we must speak out. Not in the way that I shared with you earlier, but we must declare God's word for a particular situation. We must put our faith on the line. Why did so many of my prayers go unanswered? Why did my petitions pour out in a torrent, while my answers came back in a trickle? Why did I experience weeks of silence from God? It really is simple. I had to come to the realization that I spoke with my words and not God's words.

Our words may express a wish or a hope, but God's words express a divine intention which God will back up. That is where prayer becomes trusting God's word.

"As the rain and the snow come down from heaven and return nor hither but water the earth, giving seed to the sower and bread to the eater, so shall My words be that go forth from My mouth. It shall not return to Me empty, but it shall accomplish what I purpose." Isaiah 55:10-11.

If we want to have intimacy with God in our prayer life, then we must come to the place where we speak not our words, but God's words. Then the word of our prayers on earth, are an echo of the words already spoken in heaven by God. Jesus said, "I do nothing on my own authority, but speak as the Father taught me." John

8:28. That was why His prayers were so effective. He spoke God's words.

We can do God's works.

If we have started out thinking God's thoughts and followed through to speaking God's words, chances are that we have gotten ourselves into an impossible situation. Right here is where a lot of prayer answers get lost. We see the impossible situation and push the panic button. Believe me over the past few months during this trial, I have done this many times. "Must have made a mistake somewhere." "This is an impossible situation." The tragedy is, at this point the prayer is as good as answered. All it needs now, is that we do what is possible and allow God to do what is impossible … and to trust him to do it. The do what is possible, may be a small commitment of some sort on our part. Not enough to do the whole job, but the full extent of what we are able to do. It's the story of the little boy with the loaves and fishes. All that was possible for him to do, was give them to Jesus. But it was all God needed to release the miracle that is still being talked about 2000 years later. In other words, it's not the popular phrase WWJD, "what would Jesus do," but the phrase, "what is Jesus doing." Doing God's works, means to do everything that is possible and to trust God to do the rest.

I have learned that prayer is an effective way of releasing much of our struggles, turning instead to His almighty power as our source of strength. I didn't know how much God would do until I learned and made the decision to trust Him completely. The reality of the third Proverb has become alive in my heart. "Trust in the Lord with all of your heart and lean not unto your own understanding. In all your ways, acknowledge Him and he will guide your path."

41

How blessed is the man who has "a heart for prayer."

How blessed is the man who has "a heart for the Master's use."

PERSONAL REFLECTIONS

What do I think what God is asking of me as to the daily time I commit to prayer?

Am I taking time to hear what He is saying to me?

Am I willing to move from "Mediocrity" to "having a Heart for the Master's use"?

How will I do this?

Am I willing to share this experience with others?

NOTES

A HEART ... FOR THE MASTER'S USE ... IS A HEART FOR WORSHIP

What do you think of when you see the word worship? Does it bring to mind a picture of a gothic cathedral, complete with pipe organ, robed choir, candles and pews?

Or do you see a quiet spot up in the mountains, perhaps sitting on a rock by a fast moving stream, enjoying the silence as a time of reflection. Maybe you see yourself in the middle of a contemporary Sunday morning service, with the praise team leading the entire congregation in a chorus of joyful singing. Perhaps it's none of those pictures, just something more routine, like sitting quietly at your dining room table with your Bible and a hot cup of coffee on an early winter morning.

Well, if any of those mental images sounded like worship to you, here's some good news, you are right, it is yes to all of the above!

As I shared in the beginning, each man is a unique creation of God so since each worshiper is different so is each experience different.

"For we are to God, the fragrance of Christ among those who are perishing." 2 Cor. 2:15.

When we give ourselves to God in worship, we are sharing the fragrance with Him and with others. As I said, each experience is different as each worshiper is different. We are not required to duplicate each other's experiences, but we are expected to give the same quality time and devotion to the Lord.

We must focus on God, not an experience. We must be sincere, open and honest with Him. We must give our best to do so because we love Him. We must look beyond events and experiences to see God and the work He has for us to do. We must be willing to pay the price to get to know God better. The wonder of God must humble us and excite us.

Sometimes I go to church to worship as one of His sheep, desperately needing the care of the Shepherd. "We are His people and the sheep of His pasture." Psalm 100:3. At other times, I worship as a member of the body, seeking to draw from Him, the spiritual energy I need to carry on through this time of restoration so that I will be available to minister to others in the body.

Yes, there are occasions when I share in worship as a soldier in His army, wounded from the battles, struggles and temptations of the previous week and as I walk the Calvary road to praise Him during those moments, there are many. There are also those times and how I wish there were more of them, when I simply love Him as part of His bride, and experience the inner joy and satisfaction that spiritual love can give. As the song does say, "I will give you all my worship, I will give you all my praise, you alone I long to worship, you alone are worthy of my praise."

I learned a lesson unexpectedly from a close friend recently and I want to share it with you, as I believe that it is something we have all experienced in different ways, if not the same.

I was sitting next to him in church one Sunday and I noticed that he was distant from worship. I also was reminded at the moment that he was separated from his wife and they still were attending our church and in fact, attending the same service each Sunday. He on one side of the sanctuary and she on the other. He would watch her frequently and it seemed an obsession with him that she would notice him. He shared with me later that he had the desire to sit with her, but could not at the moment and that it was hard to worship.

It was a distraction for him. God touched my heart to ask if "her presence was more important to him during the service then that of God's presence." He thought for a moment and after a serious blush said, "No, but how can I prevent this from happening and become involved in worship." For some reason my answer was simple. I said, "go to the other service."

We both realized then that the lesson God was telling both of us was that our total emotions must be part of worship and not to prevent worship. Otherwise they are a distraction and a major part of us is not yielded to the Lord.

Richard Mayhue put it in a wonderful perspective when he wrote, "Worship involves the highest privilege and the most exalted of experiences. It is the apex of Christian living. Worship fuels intimacy with God and heightens our commitment to God's kingdom purpose."

Brothers, I have learned that worship is my response of all that I am in…mind…emotion…and body…to all that God says and does. I pray that your heart will be open to the same lesson.

He defined worship for us.

When you consider all the words used for worship in both the Old and the New Testaments and when you put the meanings together, you find that worship involves both ATTITUDES (awe, reverence, respect) and ACTIONS (bowing, praising, serving). True worship is balanced and involves the MIND, the EMOTIONS and the WILL. It must reach deep within and be motivated by love and it must lead to obedient actions to glorify God and God alone.

Allow me to place a thought in your mind that will help amplify what is shared above. I am about to tell you something that you may find hard to believe. You don't have to agree with me but I would like you to consider it with me.

Have you ever been in a situation that someone did something just for you out of love and your response was that you couldn't believe that it was just done out of love and just for you. Well here goes.

If you were the only person on earth, the earth would look exactly the same. The Grand Canyon and the Himalayas would still have their drama, the sunsets in Hawaii would still be breathtaking and the Caribbean would still have its charm. The sun would still nestle behind the Rockies in the evenings and spray light on the desert in the mornings. If you were the sole pilgrim on this globe, God would not diminish its beauty one degree.

Because He did it all for you." Find such love hard to believe? Well that's OK. Remember the Cross. He did it just for you. Remember the song shared earlier. "I will give You all my worship, I will give You all my praise, You alone I long to worship, You alone are worthy of my praise."

He and He alone when it comes to worship is deserving of all our heart…our mind…and our emotions.

The Bible tells us that everything was designed by God to worship Him and to praise Him.

"You alone are Lord. You made the heavens, even the highest heavens and all their starry host, the earth and all that is on it, the seas and all that is in them. You give life to everything and the multitudes in Heaven worship you." Nehemiah 9:6.

In the Gospel of John, we see an important reference to worship in the earthly experience of Christ. Jesus had been involved in some intense ministry over a period of several months. It's hard work to preach, teach, travel and spend time with a bunch of guys who just don't seem to get it. I think of some of our worship leaders at times in this context. They try so hard to lead and at times with no heartfelt response. Jesus worshiped the Father daily in what He did as easily as He ate, walked, spoke and slept. It was His CHARACTER … it was His COUNTENANCE.

He had ministered to those who were hostile and to those who were jealous, because their leader John the Baptist was decreasing in fame and influence while Jesus was increasing, just as John had foretold. Plus, there were the Pharisees who were so jealous that it was necessary for Jesus to leave Judea.

Let's wander over to John 4, the story of Jesus and the Samaritan woman at the well.

Tired and perhaps a bit weary of heart, Jesus sat Himself at Jacob's well. A Samaritan woman came to draw water. In spite of the racism of the day between the Jews and Samaritans, Jesus asked this woman for a drink of water. A conversation took place as she addressed the long standing controversy between the Jews and the Samaritans over the correct place to worship. Jesus cut past the issues of class, culture, race, and denomination to say, "God is Spirit, and those who worship Him must worship in Spirit and Truth." John 4:24 ... In those words He defined worship for us.

Let me share a worship experience with you that God used for me to see and understand His Glory and most of all His loving presence.

I recently had a conversation with Him and it was not to my liking. I am not saying that His response to my boldness was wrong, just that it was not to my liking. I was venting to Him and with a tone of voice that if my disobedient child had spoken to me as such, I would have given a spanking. I was in my truck crying and feeling sorry for myself and feeling loneliness and all of the other things that make a good pity party. I screamed at Him, "Are you really there? Do you even hear me? This is not healing or restoration, this is punishment. If you really hear me, then show me something that is of your hand." Well, I slammed to a stop in front of my house after recklessly speeding down the driveway, nose running and tears pouring out of my sorry eyes. I stepped out of the truck, door slamming and looked up at the sky to yell at Him some more. What I saw stunned me. I had never seen what my eyes were wide open at since I was a child living in northern Canada. I have never in my 33 years of living in North Carolina seen this as it is not part of a southern sky. It was the Milky Way in all its splendor. That white ribbon of trillions of stars winding through the night sky. I stood in awe. I raised my hands and said, "Lord only you could have made something as beautiful as that." I went into the house to dry my nose and tears and opened the back door to see it again and it wasn't there. I changed into my robe and went out front again where I had seen it and there it was. More beautiful than I had remembered from a few minutes before. I stayed outside a good thirty minutes just singing praises and thanking God for not spanking me…but showing me His love and faithfulness.

I felt God speak to my heart and say "now Ken, go to bed and rest for you and I have begun our walk." It has been an upward climb since then. At times a step back, but always two steps forward.

"And when the living creatures give glory and honor and thanks to Him who sits on the throne, to Him who lives forever and ever, the twenty four will fall down before Him who sits on the throne, saying, 'Worthy are you our Lord and our God, to receive glory and honor and power, for You did create all things and because of Your will, they existed and were created.'" Rev. 4.

Worship is the highest and noblest act.

If you could see God at this moment, you would completely understand how worthy He is of worship, that you would instinctively fall on your face and worship Him. That's the kind of worship we read about all through the book of Revelation. Worship is the highest and noblest act that any man can do.

When men worship, God is satisfied. When you worship, you are fulfilled.

Think about this. Why did Jesus come? He came to make worshipers out of rebels. In my little story on the previous page, was I not a rebel? We who were once self-centered had to be completely changed so that we could shift our attention outside of ourselves and become vessels … able to worship Him.

Let me share this thought with you. "As we learn to have a heart for worship, the more we will know about God, then the more logical worship becomes."

How is it possible to worship God publicly once a week, when we don't worship Him privately throughout the week? Can we expect the flames of our worship of God to burn brightly in public on the Lord's Day, when they barely flicker for Him in secret on other days? Is it because we do not worship well in private that our corporate worship experience dissatisfies us? Is it because the words from our mouths in private are not the same words we speak in church?

I have experienced that. I love to sing and am considered to have a good voice. One day while I was in church, praising, God spoke to my heart and said to me that He didn't want the same mouth praising Him, that spoke differently during the week. He was bringing to my attention my sincerity.

I now sometimes wonder that when we get to heaven, will God call us aside to let us see what we could have accomplished if only we had taken the time to listen to His voice about our call to worship him.

Jesus said, "Take my yoke upon you and learn from me, for I am gentle and humble in heart; and you will find rest for your souls. For my yoke is easy and my load is light." Matt.11:29-30.

With that scripture in mind, let me suggest this to you.

Worship is not a burden…worship is gentleness. Worship is not tiresome…worship is restful. Worship is not hard work…worship is fun. Worship is not for some of us…worship is for all of us.

How Godly is the man who will lift his hands to the Lord and say from the bottom of his heart, "to Him who sits on the throne and unto the Lamb, be all blessing and honor and glory and power, forever and ever."

Loving…learning…worshiping.

No longer "a life we fail to live" … but "a heart of a worshiping man." "A heart for the Master's use."

PERSONAL REFLECTIONS

What do I think what God is asking of me as to the daily time I commit to worship?

Am I taking time to hear what He is saying to me?

Am I willing to move from "Mediocrity" to "having a Heart for the Master's use"?

How will I do this?

Am I willing to share this experience with others?

NOTES

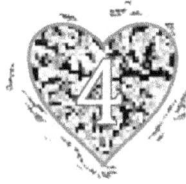

A HEART...FOR THE MASTERS USE
...IS A HEART
"FOR COMMUNICATING OUR FAITH"

Loving … learning … worshiping … wow, what a way to end a chapter and to begin another. Again the 2 Timothy 1:12 scripture comes to mind and I find myself changing that word "Know'' to "Amazed" one more time, for how can one be amazed about someone or something and not excitedly talk about them.

Earlier I shared of God's creation and His undying love for us not to change it even if we were the only living creature on this planet. It is this love that we who are amazed by this that needs to be shared.

Let me begin with a statement that I hope will touch your hearts to give you that desire to communicate your faith.

"I believe that deep in the heart of man, there is an emptiness that nothing of this world can fill. That emptiness makes it impossible to love. We who know the love of Christ, have an obligation to share that with those who do not. We are to remind them that He loves them and that His love is real as He died for them. We are to let them know that if they allow their hearts to be opened, that He will fill that emptiness forever. For "He is the same, yesterday … today … and forever."

Presenting the Gospel to an unbeliever is not an opportunity for a Christian to show off how much theology he knows. People want answers in a form they can understand. The purpose of communicating our faith is to gain a brother or sister and not to carve a notch in our evangelistic belts. I know that sounds silly, but let us not try to capture prey. Practice explaining the plan of salvation and the undying love of Christ with the simplest of terms possible. Make it clear.

Men, our lives and our message must complement each other rather than conflict. People will notice the differences if they exist and may even ask about it.

Again Jesus didn't use evangelistic formulas. He simply said "Take my yoke upon you and learn from me, for I am gentle and humble in heart; and you will find rest for your souls. For my yoke is easy and my load is light." Matt. 11:29-30.

Now how do we go about communicating with excitement. Let me put in earthly terms that we are familiar with. The day you met your wife or fiancé there was an excitement that made you have a desire to talk about her with friends and even family. As you got to know her better that excitement grew and so did the time you spent sharing about her. What you spoke of helped convince that she was the right person for you to spend the rest of your life with. When you finally introduced them to her and as time went by, your friends and family saw that she was the person that you were proud of and who had brought fulfillment to your life.

So is that excitement in communicating our faith. You share it with excitement and in a positive manner. Just as you love her and can't help talking about her, so it should be in your presenting Christ. You love Him and therefore want to tell everyone what He has done and will do.

Your desire to talk of the love of your life didn't result from your taking a course titled "How to tell others about your love for your wife." No, it's a natural outflow of your love relationship. Likewise, we don't have to take a class on evangelism in order to communicate what naturally flows from our hearts concerning the amazement we have about Jesus Christ. We should prefer it to let it be a normal, natural part of our daily lives.

Let me state the truth in unmistakable terms…. The key issue in talking about our faith, is to work on a growing and dynamic relationship with Christ. If that growing is happening, then we won't be able to keep from talking about Him.

A personal relationship with Christ will make us a powerful witness for Christ.

Our lifestyle is our witness.

However, our witnessing doesn't end with our voice and our words, it truly starts with the way we live.

Let me confess something to you. I went to church weekly, was part of a small group and even a deacon at times. Yet my witness outside of that environment was not a lifestyle that complimented Christ. I was a phony. Yes, I knew how to talk the talk when it suited me, but I certainly wasn't walking the walk. To be honest, I spent more time "saying" I was a good husband and a Godly man, than I did in "being" a good husband and a Godly man.

There is absolutely no way to effectively explain the Gospel if our lifestyle does not back up what we are saying. To use a term earlier used in this study, we must have integrity and character. Integrity and character demand that we live by the principles and guidelines set forth in God's word.

Remember the Apostle Peter's words… "but sanctify Christ as Lord in your hearts, always being ready to make a defense to everyone who asks you to give an account for the hope that is in you, yet with gentleness and reverence." 1 Peter 3:15.

This scripture can best be made alive in the following story that I have read in a Promise Keepers handbook.

A young man applied for a position with a large company. Presenting himself for his final interview with the Vice-President of the firm, the interviewer addressed him and said the following while handing him a sheet of paper and a pencil. "Before I begin this interview, I want you to write on this paper, three words that best describe your character. But before you begin, I want you to know that I have asked the same of your references and I have their answers before me this day."

Well the core of this story is this. If someone was to ask of us the same question, would one of the words that we would write or that others would write be "Godly." Until recently, in my case, absolutely not.

Does this give you something to think about?

The Christians in Peter's day, were being persecuted for simply being Christians. With the fear of torture hanging over them, it's easy to imagine that many believers went private with their faith. No one would notice anything different about them, so they weren't bothered by the persecutors. Yet others lived in a way that demonstrated hope. These people aroused such curiosity, that the non-Christians were constrained to ask them, "Why do you act the way you do? You're different. I want to know what makes you the way you are." That's lifestyle evangelism ... people seeing a life of integrity and character.

Jesus interacted with people. He didn't use evangelistic formulas, but rather reached out to them. He was willing to touch lepers when other people wouldn't even stand next to them. He met folks on their own turf, asked them questions and ... listened ... as they answered.

Many Christians today do not have non-Christian friends. If we are going to reach people of this generation, it will be only on their turf. They won't come to us!

We should prepare ourselves to discuss our faith, but nothing can replace personal interaction in the lives of others. The Lord can work through such relationships. In this process our own relationship with Christ must be kept fresh. Otherwise, we can end up offering sterile concepts about God, rather than dynamic stories of what he is doing ... right now.

It reminds me of that little arm bracelet we see around. WWJD. It's not about "what would Jesus do?" but our life style should show "what Jesus is doing."

Listening without judging.

Many nonbelievers are afraid of, or put off by traditional approaches to evangelism. At the same time they are hungry for Christian individuals to love them sincerely. That means … listening without judging and treating them as regular people, not as potential converts and a notch in our evangelistic gun belt. In this way, we earn the right to speak.

We often underestimate the power of a life well lived. I had lived mine with the thought that I was as significant to God's plan as a cloudy day. How wrong I was.

But let's be careful on this issue as there is a danger of becoming lazy, so we must not allow the concept of "letting my life speak" to become an excuse for not telling people about Christ.

The progression of 1 Peter 3:15, if we truly live for Christ, should prompt people to ask about it, so we should be then ready and willing to respond.

Witnessing may simply mean stating that you are a believer in Jesus. Many of us have a preconceived notion of verbal witnessing as being fairly confrontational. But that isn't necessarily so.

I personally, am beginning to become more comfortable around people at work and other places and in seeing the opportunity to tell them about Christ or simply offer to pray with them over a situation. But the important thing is that in some easy clear way, people hear and see about Jesus from me.

I often wonder now, how many times that my having felt insignificant to God's plan and feeling unqualified, has prevented me from opportunities of telling others about Christ.

There is no telling of what has been missed.... Mr. Kimball knows what I mean.

Mr. Kimball lived more than a hundred years ago. In 1858, while teaching a Sunday school class, he led to Christ a shoe clerk in Boston. That shoe clerk named Dwight Moody, became the evangelistic founder of the Moody Bible Institute that continues to this day. In 1879, while preaching in England, Moody awakened the evangelistic zeal in the heart of a pastor of a small church. That pastor, Fredrick B. Meyer, came to an American college campus and led to Christ a student. That student, Wilbur Chapman, began working in area YMCA's and through his outreach in those associations, he hired a former baseball player to further evangelistic work for him. The baseball player, named Billy Sunday, led thousands to Christ himself.

One time he held a crusade in Charlotte, North Carolina, where some men got so excited about evangelism, that they decided to invite another evangelist to Billy Sunday's Charlotte campaign. That evangelist, named Mordecai Hamm, led a series of meetings in which a boy trusted Jesus as his Savior. That boy, named ... Billy Graham ... has led tens of thousands of people to Christ.

Only eternity, will reveal the tremendous impact, that one school teacher, Mr. Kimball had on the lives of others.

Learning of the love of Christ is not for some of us ... it is for all of us.

It is no longer "a life we fail to live" … but a "heart for communicating our faith."

PERSONAL REFLECTIONS

What do I think what God is asking of me as to my communicating my faith?

Am I taking time to hear what He is saying to me?

Am I willing to move from "Mediocrity" to "having a Heart for the Master's use"?

How will I do this?

Am I willing to share this experience with others?

NOTES

"IT'S ... A ... WE THING"

Have you ever lived in a house best described as a "Fixer-upper? "As a matter of fact I have. My wife used to kid me and say that God loves me, but she had a plan for me for the rest of my life ... fixing up the house so that it's presentable.

It wasn't long before I finally realized that after having so many uncompleted projects, that it wasn't enough just to think about what had to be done, but I actually had to get in there and do it.

For some of us guys, our Spiritual lives are a lot like a "fixer-upper." In my case, it was ... a total demolition and rebuild.

I hope that after sharing in the previous lessons of Bible reading, Prayer time, Praise and Worship and Communicating our Faith that you will agree that there is some "fixing-upper" to do.

What I am about to share with you, is not about me.... It's a "we" thing so I am asking all of us to put in the time, energy, resources, encouragement, and the desire, to make the transformation of "a life we fail to live" into a daily reality of "having a heart for the Master's use."

There is nothing, that I could ever share with you, out of the hurt, pain and sorrow that I have experienced and even repentance, that God has not already wanted to show you.

There is nothing that I could ever encourage you to take to Him, that He will not understand. He will receive your concerns and struggles with Love and Grace.

73

"Oh, Wounded Healer, Broken One, we give You all the broken pieces of our lives and ask that You put them all together and make us whole."

Again, this testimony is not about me, "it's a we thing." Men, we need each other! The words of God, "it's not good for man to be alone," extend well beyond the marriage relationship. One Sunday as I was walking into a church that I had visited before, I heard a familiar song being played by the worship team. I started to realize why the song was familiar …it was the theme from an old television show and not just any T.V. show, but "Cheers." The Pastor used it in a way to illustrate his theme. "The church is supposed to be a place of community, a place of family," he began. "The world has many counterfeits and counterparts, but the Body of Christ has the reality." As he continued to develop his point, he chose the words to the theme song to drive it home. The church should be the place "where everybody knows your name."

Scripture describes the church in relational terms such as a body, a family and a household. If we are part of this family household, then we need each other. Yet many of us are more interested in pursuing programs than in pursuing relationships. I don't know anywhere in the Bible where God commands us to run better programs. He does however, emphasize caring for one another. Whether we're considering widows and orphans, the mission field or those in ministry, the clear idea is that … we need each other.

It's Moses with his Joshua and Jethro. It's David with his Jonathan. It's Paul and Barnabas and the group that traveled with them…. "It's you and me."

It's knowing that we are not alone in our stand for Christ or even during times of strife or turmoil. The Lord will use others in the body of Christ to help us walk with Him.

I could have never come this far in my healing and restoration without some caring brothers and sisters and their commitment of encouragement, prayers and communication on a consistent basis and the love of Christ that showed in their character. A closeness has developed between us that I can truly say, "that when one of us weeps, the others taste salt."

The truth is, that there were days when I was just tired of it all. The illness, the loneliness and all the other ingredients of a pity party, but there were brothers and sisters that I could call upon who would walk me through those moments.

Because of them, Phil. 1:12 has become a reality for me. "Now I want you know brethren, that my circumstances have turned out for the greater progress of the Gospel." What I have learned from, "It's a we thing," is, "If therefore there is any encouragement in Christ, if there is any consolation of love, if there is any fellowship of the Spirit, any affection and compassion, make my joy complete, by being of the same mind, maintaining the same love, united in one spirit, intent on one purpose. Do nothing from selfishness or empty conceit, but with humility of mind, let each of you regard one another as more important than himself. Do not merely look out for your own personal interests, but also for the interests of others. Have this attitude in yourselves which was also in Christ Jesus." Phil. 2:1-5.

There are two key words in this scripture that I want to zero in on: "selfishness" and "attitude." Earlier I shared about my fixer-upper house. My "attitude" was one of delaying my responsibilities as also was my "selfishness" in my time that I felt needed to be awarded to more important things.

May I share with you a true story that God led me through one day pertaining to "my selfishness and attitude."

I was complaining to Him again as I had so many times before about an area of my life that he was dealing with and the fact that I didn't like how He was handling it and why it was taking Him so long to correct it for me......hmm.

He brought the first Psalm to my heart. Oh I knew it very well and felt that it described me perfectly.

How blessed is the man who does not walk in the counsel of the wicked or stand in the path of sinners or sit in the seat of scoffers, but his delight is in the law of the Lord. And in His law he meditates day and night. And he will be like a tree, firmly planted by streams of water that bears its fruit in its season and its leaf does not wither. And in whatever he does he prospers."

Now you want to know about selfishness and attitude, wait until you hear this. I thought for a moment and my response was exactly as follows.

"Lord, how dare you compare me to a tree in this manner. I am a man, created in your image, with thoughts, feelings, hurts, and I even bleed and cry at times. A tree is just a stupid piece of wood that stands there, no feelings, its leaves fall all over my yard and I even pay to have them raked up. It just stands there and you are comparing me to that." Well, I now know that I have a loving Father and He answered me with that love in this manner.

He said, "Kenneth," and when I heard Kenneth and not son, I knew that I was in for a spiritual come-to-Jesus lesson. Why I am still here today and not cast in some hole somewhere I don't know.

I could hear Him now. "Well, Michael and Gabriel, here is that Rahal guy again. He has his hackles up and thinks he's strong but he's stubborn as usual. Get some of the boys as we will be doing battle with him today so let's just break him and show him love."

He lovingly, but firmly said this to my heart. "Yes, Kenneth, I did create you in my image, but I also created the tree. Yes, the tree stands there, but while it stands, it adds beauty to my landscape that I created. Its branches and leaves give shade and shelter to those who need it. It provides a home for my squirrels and birds and a playhouse for children. But it has another use. It can die and allow its wood to be used to build and restore beautiful things. When I heard this, I knew I was in trouble, as you see I am a woodworker, and I use wood to build and restore beautiful things.

Then in the lesson He was wanting to show me, God reminded me of a time when a client called and needed some immediate repairs to their home and they needed them done quickly. When I arrived at their residence, I saw that the repairs were more that what they were willing to do and all they wanted was a "quick fix" cosmetically as they were expecting guests and just wanted to make the house presentable. Against my advice, they had the quickies done and a year later called me back to do them again, spending more money than needed and never taking my advice … and at what a terrible cost.

Again, He reminded me of another client who called me, listened to my counsel, had plans drawn and we did the restoration while maintaining the "integrity and original character and beauty of the home."

Now in His timing, He reminded me of my own life. For years, whenever I had a struggle or conflict or strife, I went for the quick fix. Oh yes, I said a few "our fathers" asking in prayer, but they mostly were gimmie, gimmie, gimmies, not listening, but wanting what I wanted, never adhering to counsel or good advice, only when it was convenient and never for a lasting period. I spent all of my time, making my personality on the outside look good so that people would like me and feel comfortable around me, never spending proper time to develop character and integrity ... and at what a terrible cost.

With this picture, restoration and healing began. God was saying to me, "Son, I want you to expose yourself to me this day. To open your heart so that I can be a part of all your life. Allow me to take the "new wood" and restore what is damaged inside of you to the original beauty that I had created. Trust me so that we can do this together. I am your God who does not repair personalities, but I am the one who will build and restore lasting integrity and character.

Well, here's that "it's a we thing" again ... this time Him and me and He is asking for my trust. I hope brothers that perhaps you can identify with how I felt.

TRUST!

I felt like the Israelites in Num. 13 and 14, when Caleb and Joshua were encouraging them to go into the promised land, even though the reports from the leaders were discouraging. Their focus on the people was, "trust the Lord."

As long as it seemed good for them, as I have done many times in my own life, they kept God's word and "appeared" to desire Him....does this ring a bell? But if obedience meant going in a direction that wasn't pleasing to my flesh, I complained and stood back coveting the excuses I had found for not going forward with the call that God had placed in my life. In Num. 14:1-3, the words, "would it not be better for us," painted a clear picture on their hearts. "For out of the abundance of the heart, the mouth speaks." Matt. 12:34.

I guess I can confess, and perhaps you can too, that like them, my core motivation for living was made evident by my behavior and words spoken under pressure. It was for myself. My focus was on my own life, and not "God's Heart."

A real word of encouragement is found in the Living Bible. It is Eph. l:18 and is as follows. "I pray that the eyes of your heart will be opened, so that you will see part of the future he has called you to share." With this word, it is my hope that we all can realize it is time to quit hanging our heads in repentance for "the life we failed to live" but to lift our heads in His forgiveness so that we can have a clear vision of the plan he has for us. It is that simple action that can cause us to have a "heart for the Master's use." At times I have felt like David. Even though he had plotted, was adulterous and murdered, he was repentant. I was encouraged by his prayer in Psalm 51 and knew that even though I hadn't committed adultery or murdered someone, my sins were no different and just as grave, for they had sent my Savior to the cross.

So in not wanting to be part of "a common tragedy" any longer and wanting to change my life from the one "I had failed to live," I began each day to share in David's prayer.

"Create in me a clean heart O Lord and renew a right spirit within me. Cast me not away from your presence and take not your Holy Spirit from me. Restore unto me the joy of Your salvation and uphold me with your Spirit free. Then I will teach men your ways and sinners will be converted to you."

Well, brothers, that is my prayer and yes, I will admit, by begging God to "take my hall of shame and turn it into His hall of fame," it does sound like a bargain with the Lord, but I had no choice.

I had placed myself in that situation. It was like being in the middle of a swamp, realizing that you are up to your butt in snakes and alligators, not remembering that your original plan was to drain the swamp.

You may ask, "Well, Ken, how did you get there?" Remember what I said earlier. I thought the scripture had read, "I can do all things through Ken Rahal who strengthens me." One simple but strong words my friends: "PRIDE."

As I began to do this as I hope you will, join me in seeing that God truly does have a plan for our life and that he will always be there for us to reach forward for His hand and bail us out of the swamp.

That can be best stated in this scripture. "Not that I have already obtained it, or have already become perfect, but I press on in order that I may lay hold of that for which I was also laid hold of for Christ Jesus. Brethren I do not regard myself as having laid hold of it, yet on thing I do, forgetting what lies behind and reaching forward for what lies ahead, I press on toward the goal for the prize of the upward call of God in Christ Jesus. "Phil. 3:12, 13, 14. YOU CAN DO IT.

With that scripture in mind, and with the help of your imagination, I ask you to think about what is possible when a man gets serious about Spiritual Growth.

Can you see a man whose life corresponds to his heart? Deep inside he really wants to love and serve the Lord.

Now through the addition of some important characteristics, he demonstrates his love for God on the outside as well.

Don't misread these words, however, for I am not suggesting that you attempt all of what has been said and shared herein immediately, or that you create some sort of "sanctified to-do list."

That won't work. You will experience Spiritual Growth for about one week, then you will be too overwhelmed to make it happen, canning the whole process. No, I am suggesting that you incorporate the following one at a time. As each one grows and develops, take a new one.

It will begin the process of developing "a heart for the Masters use."

HE LOVES HIS BIBLE ... he's committed to reading it, studying it, listening to sermons, memorizing important passages and even meditating on it. So he misses a day here and there, but it is far more consistent than he has ever been in the past and he as well as others, can see the difference in his life.

HE HAS LEARNED THE VALUE OF PRAYER ... in a personal way. He can pick up the phone and talk to the Lord whenever he wants. He's learning the importance of praying as

Jesus would pray. Discerning the will of God in his life is clearer now that he's disciplined in his prayer life.

HE HAS A NEW APPRECIATION FOR WORSHIP ...

It's more than a Sunday ritual for him. Now it's a rich, full and vibrant part of his life. He knows the value of corporate worship and it has made a difference in the way he relates to God.

HE WANTS TO BE A MORE EFFECTIVE WITNESS

... learning to communicate his faith has become important to him. So he's doing his best to live a life that causes people to see the hope in him. When the opportunity presents itself, he has also learned to take the time to communicate his faith verbally. Does this guy look familiar to you? Well if you have taken the time to apply to your life what I have been talking about, I have good news for you. That person is you! That's right ... it's you. There has been absolutely nothing that I have shared with you that you can't do. Men who succeed at practicing Spiritual Growth do not have a "Super S" sewn on their chests, nor do they have a cape that flutters in the breeze as they fly over tall buildings.

It's not a Superman thing ... it's an Ordinary man thing. Therein lies the encouragement. Ordinary men like you and me can see the difference in our lives as we allow the Holy Spirit to help us make Spiritual Growth, a reality.

IT'S GOD'S OWN WORK.

Men, let us make a commitment to remind each other of the greatness and glory of the life in which God gives us to live. It is nothing less than the work of bringing back to God, people in whom we share the excitement of our first love relationship with Him. But as we see that it is God's own work that we are to perform, that He works it through us, that in doing it, His Glory rests on us and we glorify Him.

We will count it our joy to give ourselves to live completely for Him. God's work must be done in God's way and in God's power. Our joy in God's work will be greater, the more we learn, the more we understand and the more we submit ourselves to His will to become "useful for the Master's use."

As we agree and strive and admit that it is "a we thing," we become vessels for Christ to use. In every work we do it is to be Christ using us and working through us. The sense of being a humble servant, a Godly man, dependent on the Master's guidance, working under the Master's eye, instruments used by Him and His mighty power, lies at the heart of effectual service.

It keeps up that blessed consciousness of the work being all His, which leads a man who has a "heart for the Master's use" to become more humble the more he is used.

Yes, it is a "we thing" for I encourage you in all that we have studied in this book "to proclaim Him, admonishing every man and teaching every man with all wisdom, that we may present every man complete in Christ. And for this purpose also I labor, striving according to His power, which mightily works within me." Col. 1:28-29. A personal relationship with Christ and an entire surrender to His disposal, a dependent waiting to be used by him, a joyful confidence that He will use us.

That is how we build integrity and character, the most important gift to man from God, next to our salvation.

Such is the joy of leaving behind that "common tragedy" and moving from "the life we fail to live" to having "a heart for the Master's use."

"To Him who sits on the throne and unto the lamb, be all blessing and honor and glory and power, forever and ever."

It's a we thing.

www.ingramcontent.com/pod-product-compliance
Lightning Source LLC
Chambersburg PA
CBHW071829020426
42331CB00007B/1669